DATE DUE			

GAYLORD M2

Also by Anne Rockwell:

The Three Bears & 15 Other Stories

THE THREE SILLIES

and 10 Other Stories to Read Aloud

told and illustrated by

Anne Rockwell

THOMAS Y. CROWELL
NEW YORK

For my three children

Library of Congress Cataloging in Publication Data
Rockwell, Anne.
The old woman and her pig, and 10 other stories.
CONTENTS: The old woman and her pig.—The three
sillies.—The travels of a fox.—The milkmaid and the
bucket of milk.—Lambikin. [etc.]
1. Tales [1. Folklore] I. Rockwell, Anne F.
PZ8.1.046 1979 398.2′08 [E] 78-13901
ISBN 0-690-04889-0 ISBN 0-690-04891-2 lib. bdg.

CONTENTS

THE OLD WOMAN AND HER PIG

An old woman was sweeping her house when she found a little crooked sixpence.

"What should I do with this sixpence?" she said to herself. "I know. I will go to market and buy a little pig."

As she was coming home, she came to a stile, but piggy wouldn't go over the stile.

She went a little farther and she met a dog. "This dog can be a help to me," she thought. So she said, "Dog, dog! Bite pig! Piggy won't go over the stile, and I shan't get home tonight."

But the dog wouldn't.

She went a little farther and she met a stick. So she said, "Stick, stick! Beat dog! Dog won't bite pig. Piggy won't get over the stile, and I shan't get home tonight."

But the stick wouldn't.

She went a little farther and she met a fire. So she said, "Fire, fire! Burn stick! Stick won't beat dog. Dog won't bite pig. Piggy won't get over the stile, and I shan't get home tonight."

But the fire wouldn't.

She went a little farther and she met some water. So she said, "Water, water! Quench fire! Fire won't burn stick. Stick won't beat dog. Dog won't bite pig. Piggy won't get over the stile, and I shan't get home tonight."

But the water wouldn't.

She went a little farther and she met an ox. So she said, "Ox, ox! Drink water! Water won't quench fire. Fire won't burn stick. Stick won't beat dog. Dog won't bite pig. Piggy won't get over the stile, and I shan't get home tonight."

But the ox wouldn't.

She went a little farther and she met a butcher. So she said, "Butcher, butcher! Kill ox! Ox won't drink water. Water won't quench fire. Fire won't burn stick. Stick won't beat dog. Dog won't bite pig. Piggy won't get over the stile, and I shan't get home tonight."

But the butcher wouldn't.

She went a little farther and she met a rope. So she said, "Rope, rope! Hang butcher! Butcher won't kill ox. Ox won't drink water. Water won't quench fire. Fire won't burn stick. Stick won't beat dog. Dog won't bite pig. Piggy won't get over the stile, and I shan't get home tonight."

But the rope wouldn't.

She went a little farther and she met a rat. So she said, "Rat, rat! Gnaw rope! Rope won't hang butcher. Butcher won't kill ox. Ox won't drink water. Water won't quench fire. Fire won't burn stick. Stick won't beat dog. Dog won't bite pig. Piggy won't get over the stile, and I shan't get home tonight."

But the rat wouldn't.

She went a little farther and she met a cat. So she said, "Cat, cat! Eat rat! Rat won't gnaw rope. Rope won't hang butcher. Butcher won't kill ox. Ox won't drink water. Water won't quench fire. Fire won't burn stick. Stick won't beat dog. Dog won't bite pig. Piggy won't get over the stile, and I shan't get home tonight."

The cat yawned and said to her, "If you will fetch me a saucer of milk, I will eat the rat."

So she went a little farther and she met a cow. When she asked for some milk, the cow said to her, "If you will go to yonder haystack and fetch me some hay, I will give you the milk."

As soon as the cow had eaten the hay, she gave the old woman the saucer of milk, and away with the saucer of milk to the cat went the old woman.

As soon as the cat had lapped up the milk, the cat began to eat the rat. The rat began to gnaw the rope. The rope began to hang the butcher. The butcher began to kill the ox. The ox began to drink the water. The water began to quench the fire. The fire began to burn the stick. The stick began to beat the dog. The dog began to bite the pig. The little piggy in a fright jumped over the stile, and the old woman got home that night.

THE THREE SILLIES

Once upon a time there was a farmer and his wife, and they had one daughter who was being courted by a gentleman. Every night he used to come for supper, and the daughter used to go down to the cellar to get a jug of cider.

One evening she went down, and she happened to look up at the ceiling while the jug was filling, and she saw a big hatchet stuck in one of the beams. It must have been there a long time, but somehow she had never noticed it before, and she began thinking.

And she thought, "Suppose we were to be married and we were to have a son, and we sent him down to the cellar to get cider, and that hatchet was to fall on his head, what a dreadful thing that would be!" And she sat down and began to cry.

Well, upstairs they began to wonder what was keeping her, so her mother went down to see. She found the daughter sitting on the bench crying and the cider running all over the floor.

"Why, whatever is the matter?" said her mother.

"Oh, mother!" said the daughter. "Look at that hatchet! Suppose my sweetheart and I got married and had a son, and we sent him down to the cellar to get cider, and that hatchet fell on his head, what a dreadful thing that would be!"

"Oh, yes, what a dreadful thing it would be!" said the mother, and she sat down alongside the daughter and started crying, too.

Then after a bit the father began to wonder why they didn't come back, and he went down to the cellar to look for himself. There the two sat crying and the cider running all over the floor.

"Whatever is the matter?" said he.

"Why," said the mother, "look at that hatchet! Just suppose our daughter and her sweetheart got married and suppose they had a son, and he came down to the cellar to get cider and that hatchet fell on his head. What a dreadful thing that would be!"

"So it would! So it would!" said the father, and sat down beside his wife and daughter and started crying, too.

Now the gentleman got tired of sitting in the kitchen all by himself, so he went down to the cellar to see what was taking so long. There sat all three, crying side by side, and the cider running all over the floor. And he ran and turned off the tap, and said, "Whatever are you three doing, sitting there crying and letting the cider run all over the floor?"

"Oh," said the father, "look at that hatchet! Suppose you and our daughter got married and suppose you had a son, and he came down to the cellar to get cider and that hatchet fell on his head!" And they all three started crying again, worse than before.

Then the gentleman burst out laughing. He pulled down the hatchet and said, "I've traveled many miles, but I've never seen three such big sillies as you before. I will start out on my travels again, and when I find three bigger sillies than you three, I'll come back and marry your daughter." So he said good-bye and set out on his travels.

Well, he traveled a long way, and he came to a house that had grass growing on the roof. A woman was trying to get her cow to go up the ladder and on to the roof to eat the grass, and the poor thing would not go. So the gentleman asked the woman what she was doing.

"Why, look!" she said. "Just look at that beautiful good grass. I'm going to get the cow up on the roof to eat it. She'll be quite safe there, for I shall tie a rope around her neck and pass it down the chimney and tie the other end to my wrist as I go about the house. That way she can't fall off the roof without my knowing it."

"Oh, you poor silly!" said the gentleman. "You should cut the grass and throw it down to the cow."

But the woman thought it easier to get the cow up than the grass down, so she pushed her and coaxed her and got her up. Then she tied a rope around the cow's neck, passed it down the chimney, and fastened the other end to her wrist. The gentleman went on his way, but he hadn't gone far when the cow tumbled off the roof and hung by the rope tied around her neck. The weight of the cow at the other end of the rope that was tied to her wrist pulled the woman up the chimney, and she stuck halfway, all smothered in soot.

Well, that was one big silly.

The gentleman journeyed on until nightfall, and he went to an inn to spend the night. The inn was so full they had to put him in a double-bedded room, and another traveler was to share the bed. The other man was a very pleasant fellow, but in the morning, when they were getting dressed, the gentleman was surprised to see the other fellow hang his trousers on the knobs of the chest of drawers and run across the room and try to jump into them. He tried over and over again and just couldn't manage it, and the gentleman wondered what he was doing it for.

At last he stopped and wiped his face with a handkerchief. "Oh, dear," he said, "I do think trousers are the most awkward clothes there are. Who could have invented such things? It takes me the best part of an hour to get into them every morning, and I get so hot and tired. How do you manage yours?"

The gentleman burst out laughing and showed him how to put them on. The other fellow was much obliged to him, for he said he never would have thought of doing it that way.

So that was another big silly.

Then the gentleman went on his travels again. He came to a village, and outside that village there was a pond, and around the pond there was a crowd of people. And they all had rakes and brooms and pitchforks reaching into the pond, and the gentleman asked what was the matter.

"Why," they said, "matter enough! Moon's tumbled into the pond, and we can't get it out!"

So the gentleman burst out laughing and told them to look up into the sky for it was only the moon's reflection in the water. But they wouldn't listen to him and abused him most shamefully, so he got away as quickly as he could.

Well, there were a whole lot of sillies bigger than the three at home. So the gentleman turned back and married the farmer's daughter, and if they didn't live happily ever after, that's got nothing to do with you or me.

One day a fox was digging behind a stump, and he found a bumblebee. The fox put the bumblebee in a bag and threw the bag over his shoulder, and he traveled.

At the first house he came to, he went in and said to the mistress of the house, "May I leave my bag here while I go to Squintum's?"

"Yes," said the woman.

"Then be careful not to open the bag," said the fox.

But as soon as he was out of sight, the woman said to herself, "Well I wonder what the fox has in his bag? I will look and see. It can't do any harm, for I will tie the bag right up again."

However, the moment she untied the string, out flew the bumblebee, and the rooster caught him and ate him all up.

After a while the fox came back. He picked up his bag, and he knew at once that his bumblebee was gone, so he said to the woman, "Where is my bumblebee?"

And the woman said, "I untied the string just to take a little peep at what was in the bag, and the bumblebee flew out, and the rooster ate him."

"Very well," said the fox. "I must have the rooster, then."

So he caught the rooster and put him in his bag and traveled.

At the next house he came to, he went in and said to the mistress of the house, "May I leave my bag here while I go to Squintum's?"

"Yes," said the woman.

"Then be careful not to open the bag," said the fox.

But as soon as he was out of sight, the woman said to herself, "Well I wonder what the fox has in his bag? I will look and see. It can't do any harm, for I will tie the bag right up again."

However, the moment she untied the string, the rooster flew out, and the pig caught him and ate him up.

After a while the fox came back. He picked up his bag, and he knew at once that the rooster was gone, and he said to the woman, "Where is my rooster?"

And the woman said, "I untied the string just to take a little peep at what was in the bag, and the rooster flew out, and the pig ate him."

"Very well," said the fox. "I must have the pig, then."

So he caught the pig and put him in his bag and traveled.

At the next house he came to, he went in and said to the mistress of the house, "May I leave my bag here while I go to Squintum's?"

"Yes," said the woman.

"Then be careful not to open the bag," said the fox.

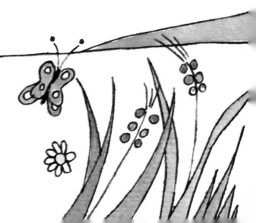

But as soon as he was out of sight, the woman said to herself, "Well I wonder what the fox has in his bag? I will look and see. It can't do any harm, for I will tie the bag right up again."

However, the moment she untied the string, the pig got out, and the woman's little boy chased him out of the house and across a meadow and over a hill, clear out of sight.

After a while the fox came back. He picked up his bag and knew at once that the pig was gone, and he said to the woman, "Where is my pig?"

And the woman said, "I untied the string just to take a little peep at what was in the bag, and the pig jumped out. Then my little boy chased him out of the house and across a meadow and over a hill, clear out of sight."

"Very well," said the fox. "I must have the little boy, then."

So he caught the little boy and put him in his bag and traveled.

At the next house he came to, he went in and said to the mistress of the house, "May I leave my bag here while I go to Squintum's?"

"Yes," said the woman.

"Then be careful not to open the bag," said the fox.

The woman had been baking cake, and when she took it from the oven, her children all gathered around her, saying, "Oh, mama, give us a piece!"

And the good smell of the cake came to the little boy in the bag, and he said, "Oh, please, give me a piece!"

Then the woman opened the bag and took the
little boy out. She put the house dog in the bag, and
the little boy ate cake and went out to play with the
other children.

After a while the fox came back. He picked up his
bag and saw that it was tied good and tight, and he
thought the little boy was safe inside.

"I have been all day on the road," said he to himself, "without a thing to eat, and I am getting hungry. I will just step off into the woods and see how this little boy in my bag tastes."

So deep into the woods he traveled. Then he sat down and untied the bag, and if the little boy had been in there, things would have gone badly with him.

But the little boy was at the house of the woman who had made the cake, and when the fox untied the bag, the house dog jumped out and ate him all up.

Perrette, the milkmaid, set out for town, wearing her prettiest dress and carrying a bucket of fresh milk on her head. As she walked along and walked along with that heavy bucket of milk, she began to daydream, and her happy thoughts made the road seem shorter and the bucket seem lighter.

"Let me see now," she said to herself. "I will sell my big bucket of fresh milk for one hundred eggs. Oooh! I know the fox will eat none of *my* little chicks for I shall hatch them inside my house. Then I will sell my chicks for a little pig. And when he grows big and fat, I'll sell him for plenty of money. I'll get such a good price for my big fat pig, I'll buy myself a cow, a bull, and a little calf. Then, soon I will have a whole herd of cattle. And, oh, how I'll dance and skip with joy when I lead my very own herd out to the morning meadows!"

And at this happy thought Perrette jumped for joy along the dusty road. Down fell the bucket of milk—and it was good-bye to cow, bull, calf, pig, chicks, eggs.

All gone!

LAMBIKIN

Once upon a time there was a little Lambikin. One day he set off to visit his Granny. He jumped and frisked and kicked with joy when he thought of all the good things he would get from her. All of a sudden, whom should he meet but a jackal. The jackal looked at Lambikin and said, "Lambikin, Lambikin! I'll eat you!"

But Lambikin only gave a little frisk, and said,

"To Granny's house I go,
Where I shall fatter grow.
Then you can eat me so."

So the jackal let Lambikin pass.

By and by he met an eagle, and the eagle said,
"Lambikin, Lambikin! I'll eat you!"

But Lambikin only gave a little frisk, and said,

> *"To Granny's house I go,*
> *Where I shall fatter grow.*
> *Then you can eat me so."*

So the eagle let Lambikin pass.

And by and by he met a tiger, and a wolf, and a dog, and all these, when they saw the tender little morsel, said, "Lambikin, Lambikin! I'll eat you!"

But to all of them Lambikin only gave a little frisk and said,

> *"To Granny's house I go,*
> *Where I shall fatter grow.*
> *Then you can eat me so."*

When, at last, he reached his Granny's house, he said, "Granny dear, I've promised to get very fat, and as one must always keep a promise, please put me in the corn bin at once."

So his Granny called him a good boy and put him into the corn bin. There the greedy little Lambikin stayed for seven days. He ate, and ate, and ate until he could scarcely waddle. Then his Granny said he was fat enough for anything and must go home. But clever little Lambikin saw that that would never do, for now he was so nice and fat, some animal would surely eat him on his way home.

"I'll tell you what you must do," said Lambikin to his Granny. "You must make me a little drumikin, and then I can sit inside and trundle along nicely, for I'm tight as a drum myself."

So his Granny made a nice little drumikin, and Lambikin curled up snug and warm in the middle and trundled away gaily. Soon he met the eagle, who called out, "Drumikin, drumikin! Have you seen Lambikin?"

And Lambikin replied,

> *"Fallen in the fire,*
> *And so will you.*
> *On little drumikin!*
> *Tum-pa, tum-too!"*

And the eagle flew away.

Lambikin trundled along, laughing to himself and singing,

"Tum-pa, tum-too!
Tum-pa, tum-too!"

Every animal and bird he met asked him the same question.

"Drumikin! Drumikin!
Have you seen Lambikin?"

And to all of them little, sly Lambikin replied,

"Fallen in the fire,
And so will you.
On little drumikin!
Tum-pa, tum-too!"

At last the jackal came limping along and looking dismal. He, too, called out,

> *"Drumikin! Drumikin!*
> *Have you seen Lambikin?"*

And Lambikin, curled up in his drumikin, replied gaily,

> *"Fallen in the fire,*
> *And so will you.*
> *On little drumikin!*
> *Tum-pa…"*

But he never got any further, for the jackal
recognized his voice and tore open the drumikin and
gobbled up Lambikin and that was the end of that.

The Tortoise and The Hare

One day the hare was boasting of how fast he could run.

"I have never yet lost a race," he said, "and I challenge any of you to race with me."

No animal said a word, but at last the tortoise said, "I accept your challenge. I will race with you."

"Ha!" said the hare, "What kind of a joke is this? You slow old plodder! You could never beat me."

"Keep your boasting for the finish," said the tortoise. "Shall we begin?"

So the other animals decided on a course and marked a finish line. Off went the tortoise and the hare. The hare leaped and ran out of sight at once. The tortoise plodded slowly on.

After a while the hare looked behind him.
Nowhere could he see the tortoise.

"Well, he'll never catch up," said the hare to
himself. "I might as well relax and take a little nap."

And the sun was so warm and the air so fresh that the hare fell fast asleep. On he slept as the tortoise plodded slowly on and on. The hare awoke just in time to see the tortoise cross the finish line.

And the other animals all shouted out, "Hooray! Slow and steady wins the race!"

Then the hare stopped boasting—for a while.

A man once had a donkey who had carried his wheat to the mill for many a year, but the donkey's strength was going for he was growing old. Then his master began to think about what to do with the old donkey, but the donkey ran away and set out on the road to Bremen.

"There," he thought, "I can surely be town musician."

When the donkey had gone some distance, he came to an old dog, lying in the road, gasping.

"Why are you gasping so, you big fellow?" asked the donkey.

"Ah," said the dog, "because I am old and weak and can no longer hunt, my master wants to kill me. So I ran away as fast as I could, but now, how will I earn my keep?"

"I am going to Bremen," said the donkey. "There I shall be town musician. Come with me. I will play the lute, and you shall beat the kettledrum."

The dog agreed, and on they went.

Before long they came to a cat, sitting in the path, with a face like three rainy days.

"Now, old puss, what has gone askew with you?" asked the donkey.

"Poor me," said the cat. "Because I am now old and my teeth are worn to stumps, I prefer to sit by the fire rather than hunt rats and mice. But my mistress wants to drown me, so I ran away. But where am I to go?"

"Come with us to Bremen," said the donkey. "You understand night music, so you can be a town musician."

The cat thought well of it, and went with them. Then the three passed a farm where a cock was crowing with all his might.

"Your crow goes through my heart," said the donkey. "What is the matter?"

"Oh, I have crowed up the sun for many mornings of many years, but now guests are coming on Sunday, and the cook intends to put me in the soup tomorrow. So I crow while still I can."

"Ah, but Old Red-Comb," said the donkey, "you had better come away with us. We are going to Bremen to be town musicians, and you with your good voice can make fine music with us."

The cock agreed and all four went on together.
They could not reach Bremen in one day, however,
and in the evening they came to a forest. Far off
through the trees they saw a little light shining, and
they thought there must be a house in the forest.

The dog said, "A few bones with some meat on
them would do me good."

So they made their way through the forest until they came to a snug little house, which was well lighted. The donkey, being biggest, looked in the window. What did he see but a table covered with good things to eat and drink and four robbers sitting there enjoying themselves. For the musicians had come upon a robbers' house.

"If only we were in there!" said the donkey.

So the animals thought of a plan to drive away the robbers. The donkey placed himself with his forefeet upon the windowsill, the dog jumped on the donkey's back, the cat climbed upon the dog, and the cock flew up and perched on the head of the cat.

And then they began to perform their music together. The donkey brayed. The dog barked. The cat miaowed, and the cock crowed so loud it broke the window glass. And the robbers jumped up in fright and ran away.

The four musicians sat down at the table and ate and drank all the good things that were left.

As soon as they finished, the four musicians put out the light and found places to sleep. The donkey lay down on some straw in the yard. The dog lay down at the back door. The cat sat by the dying fire, and the cock perched high on a beam of the roof.

When the robbers saw that the light was out in their house and all was quiet, one said, "We shouldn't have been so frightened," and he went back to examine the house.

The robber entered the house and went to light a candle. He mistook the glistening, fiery eyes of the cat for live coals, and held a match to them to light it. But the cat flew in his face, spitting and scratching. The robber was dreadfully frightened and ran to the back door, but the dog jumped up and bit his leg. As soon as he ran across the yard, the donkey gave him a good kick. And the cock began to crow, "Cock-a-doodle-doo!"

The robber ran back into the forest as fast as he could and said to the others, "Oh, there is a horrible witch sitting in our house who spat on me and scratched my face with her long claws. By the back door stands a man with a knife who stabbed me in the leg. In the yard there lies a huge monster who beat me with a club, and above the roof there sits the judge who called out, 'Cook him in the stew!' So I got away as well as I could."

After this the robbers never again dared enter the house. But it suited the Bremen town musicians so well that they did not want to leave it. So there they stayed, in comfort and friendship, in the snug little cottage for the rest of their days.

The Fox and The Crow

A sly, hungry fox was trotting along when it saw a crow flying overhead holding a big piece of yellow cheese in its beak. And the sly fox thought, "Yum! How tasty that cheese will be. And I know a way to get it for myself."

The crow perched on the branch of a tree, still holding the cheese. From down below, the fox called, "Hello, my friend. How gloriously your feathers sparkle in the morning sun. How glossy they are—so shiny and black. How I would love to hear you sing, for surely any bird with feathers so beautiful must have a voice to match."

That silly crow thought to itself, "Yes, the fox is right. I am very good-looking indeed, and just because the other birds do not like my song, *I* think it is beautiful. This fox is very intelligent, and has good taste besides." But the crow didn't sing. Not yet.

The fox called again, "No doubt your song is more lovely than the nightingale's, that drab, dull-feathered fellow. Ah, if I could only hear you sing. What music that would be!"

The silly crow croaked out its harsh, hoarse crow cry, "Caw! Caw! Caw!" And as it did so its big beak opened wide and down fell the good yellow cheese. The cheese landed right in the open mouth of that sly fox, who gobbled it down, and ran off, grinning.

So the crow had nothing to eat that day. And it sang no more.

The Lad Who Went To The North Wind

Once upon a time there was a widow who had one son, and he went out to the storehouse to fetch some oatmeal for cooking. But as he was coming back to the house, there came the North Wind, puffing and blowing. The North Wind caught up the oatmeal and blew it away. Then the lad went back to the storehouse for more, but no sooner had he come outside than the North Wind came and blew away the oatmeal with just one puff. Worse yet, the Wind did it a third time.

At this the lad got very angry, and as he thought it mean that the North Wind should behave so, he decided he'd go and find the North Wind and ask him to give back the oatmeal.

So off he went, but the way was long, and he walked and he walked, but at last he came to the North Wind's house.

"Good day," said the lad. "Thank you for coming to see us yesterday."

"Good day!" answered the North Wind in a loud, gruff voice. "Thanks for coming to see me. What do you want?"

"Oh," said the lad, "I only wished to ask you to be so kind as to let me have back that oatmeal you took from me, for my mother and I haven't much to live on. If you're to go on snapping up every morsel we have, we'll starve."

"I haven't got your oatmeal," said the North Wind, "but if you are in such need, I'll give you a cloth which will give you all the food you want if you will only say, 'Cloth, cloth, spread yourself and serve up a good dinner!'"

With this the lad was happy. But as the way was so long he couldn't get home in one day, so he stopped overnight at an inn. He went to sit down to supper, and he laid the cloth on a table and said, "Cloth, cloth, spread yourself and serve up a good dinner!"

And the cloth did.

Everyone at the inn thought this was a wonderful thing, but most of all the landlady. So when everyone was fast asleep, she took the lad's cloth and put another in its place. It looked just like the one the lad had got from the North Wind, but it couldn't serve up even a bit of stale bread.

When the lad woke, he took his cloth and went home to his mother.

"Now," said he, "I've been to the North Wind's house, and a good fellow he is. He gave me this cloth, and when I say to it, 'Cloth, cloth, spread yourself and serve up a good dinner!' I can get all the food I want."

"Seeing is believing," said his mother. "I shan't believe it until I see it."

So the lad made haste, and laid the cloth on the table. Then he said, "Cloth, cloth, spread yourself and serve up a good dinner!"

But the cloth served up nothing, not even a bit of stale bread.

"Well," said the lad, "there is nothing to do but to go to the North Wind again." And away he went.

So he walked and he walked, and late in the afternoon he came to where the North Wind lived.

"Good evening," said the lad.

"Good evening," said the North Wind in a loud, gruff voice.

"I want my rights for that oatmeal of ours you took," said the lad. "As for the cloth I got from you, it isn't worth a penny."

"I've got no oatmeal," said the North Wind. "But I'll give you a goat which gives forth golden coins whenever you say to it, 'Goat, goat, make money!'"

So the lad thought this a fine thing, but it was too
far to get home that day, so he turned in for the night
at the same inn where he had slept before.

When he was settled, he tried out the goat the
North Wind had given him and found it all right,
but when the landlord saw the goat give forth
golden coins, he changed it for an ordinary goat
while the lad slept.

Next morning off went the lad. When he got home, he said to his mother, "What a good fellow the North Wind is! Now he has given me a goat that gives forth golden coins whenever I say, 'Goat, goat, make money!'"

"All very true, I daresay," said his mother. "But I shan't believe it until I see the gold coins made."

"Goat, goat, make money!" said the lad, but the goat didn't.

So the lad went back to the North Wind and got very angry, for he said the goat was worth nothing, and he must have his oatmeal back.

"Well," said the North Wind, "I've nothing else to give you except that old stick in the corner, but it's a stick that if you say, 'Stick, stick, lay on!' lays on until you say, 'Stick, stick, now stop!'"

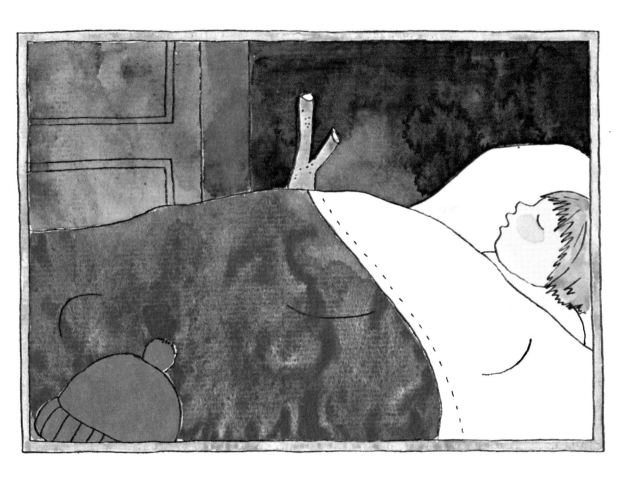

So, as the way was long, the lad turned in for the night at the same inn. By now he had pretty well guessed what had become of the cloth and the goat, so he lay down on the bed and began to snore, pretending to be asleep.

Now the landlord, who was sure the stick must be worth something, found one just like it. When he heard the lad snore, he was going to exchange the two, but just as he was about to take the stick, the lad yelled out, "Stick, stick, lay on!"

So the stick began to beat the landlord, and the landlord jumped over tables, chairs, and benches, and yelled and roared, "Oh, my! Oh, my! Bid the stick be still, and you shall have both your cloth and your goat!"

So the lad said, "Stick, stick, now stop!"

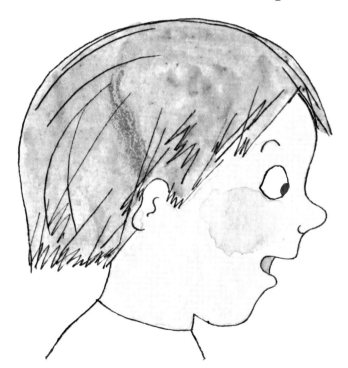

Then he took the cloth, put it in his pocket, and went home with his stick in his hand, leading the goat by a rope, and so he got his rights for the oatmeal he had lost, and if he didn't live happily ever after, that's not the fault of either you or me.

THE FROG

and

THE OX

A frog saw a big, heavy ox. "How magnificent that big ox is!" thought the frog, who was himself no bigger than a goose egg. "How I wish I were as big as that ox. How splendid I would be!"

And that little frog envied that big ox more and more each day. He puffed and panted and puffed and

panted as he tried to equal the ox in size. And as the frog did so, he said to his sister, "Look at me. Aren't I growing almost as big as the ox? Look carefully now, and tell me."

"No, no, no," said his sister.

So the little frog puffed himself up some more.

"Now look at me," he said. "I'm sure that now I'm almost as big as the ox."

But his sister said, "Not nearly."

And the little frog puffed and panted and puffed
and panted and puffed and panted until...
HE POPPED!
Poor frog. The world is full of fools.

81

THE SHEPHERD BOY

There was once upon a time a shepherd boy whose fame spread far and wide because of the wise answers he gave to every question. The king of the country heard of the shepherd boy and sent for him. Then the king said, "If you can answer three questions, I will look upon you as my own child and you shall live in the royal palace." And the boy said, "What are the three questions?"

The king said, "The first is, How many drops of water are there in the ocean?"

The shepherd boy answered, "Lord King, if you will have all the rivers on earth dammed up so that not a single drop of water runs from them into the sea until I have counted it, then I will tell you how many drops there are in the sea."

Then the king said, "The next question is, How many stars are there in the sky?"

The shepherd boy said, "Give me a big sheet of white paper and a pen." Then he made so many tiny dots on the big sheet of white paper that each one could scarcely be seen, and it was all but impossible to count them for it made one dizzy to look at them. Then the shepherd boy said, "There are as many stars in the sky as there are dots on this paper. Just count them."

But no one could.

Then the king said, "The third question is this, How many seconds of time are there in eternity?"

And the shepherd boy said, "In Lower Pomerania is the Diamond Mountain, which is two miles high, two miles wide, and two miles deep. Every hundred years a little bird comes and sharpens its beak on Diamond Mountain. When that whole mountain is worn away by this, then the first second of eternity will be over."

The king said, "You have answered the three questions like a wise man. Now you shall live with me in the royal palace and I will look on you as my own child."